BRIDGE

We hug   we need_____   we_____
cut   and   we   bleed_____   some how   we   dis-cov-er   we're
so much   like each   o-ther___   oh___   yes we are   yes we are_____   We're all
Beads   on One   String_____   ev'ry   man   ev'ry   wo-man   boy and   girl___
Beads   on One   String_____   we're one   world_____   We're all
We're all   beads   on   one   string_____   we're one   world___
we're   one_____   world.

2. You laugh, you cry, guess what? so do I
   We cough and we sneeze into the same air we all breathe
   We trust, we give, we die after we've lived
   We win, sometimes we're gonna lose
   We're wearing the same shoes.
   oh we're all...

To Elise,
With much love,
Uncle Bob & Aunt Esther

Peace!
[signature] 7-7-07

Beads on One String

Words & Music by Dennis Warner

A Minnesota resident, Dennis Warner loves spending his free time outdoors in nature. Several of his songs include references to favorite hobbies such as sailing, camping and star gazing.

On stage, he is best known for his crafty wit, skillful musicianship and the special gift of captivating the audience. Averaging over 100 concerts a year, Dennis appears not only at major theaters, clubs and festivals, but also in small town community concerts.

He has released many CD's, appeared on numerous radio and T.V. shows and received his most notable honor for song writing with an invitation to perform in concert at the Kennedy Center in Washington, D.C.

While all of his shows are family friendly, Dennis is often found doing special concerts *just for kids and others who like to have fun!*

This book evolved from Dennis' love for children and his hope for the future. To learn more about Dennis Warner, please visit his website: www.WarnerSongs.com

Illustrated by Alison Love Unzelman

Alison lives and works in a log house surrounded by trees in Minnesota with her husband and two sons, two dogs – Bear and Picasso, a cat named Lucy, many fish and several bats in the roof.

Alison has been drawing and painting for as long as she can remember. This is her first time illustrating a children's book. "How wonderful it is to illustrate a song that gives kids and families a message of love and peace with diversity. *Beads on One String* shares a truth I believe."

Forward

The idea for this song came about by visualizing a beaded necklace, with each bead representing a different person. The beads are all different sizes, shapes and colors, but all held together by the same string.

It's easy for us to notice how different we are from each other. However, if we look at how much we have in common, maybe we can build better relationships locally and even globally. **Beads on One String** is a song for all of us, kids and adults alike.

Please write or email me your comments on the book. I'd love to hear from you!

Peace,

Dennis Warner • P.O. Box 365 • Clearwater, MN 55320 USA
Email: info@WarnerSongs.com • Website: www.WarnerSongs.com

About the Beads on one String Project

By incorporating the different disciplines of music, art and social studies, The Beads on One String Project presents educators with a unique opportunity to address anti-bullying, racial, ethnic and disability issues in a fun and positive way. To learn more about how to bring this special project to your school, go to www.WarnerSongs.com/project

ISBN: 0-9747147-7-1

Published by:
MK Publishing
420 E. St. Germain
St. Cloud, MN 56304
800-551-1023
www.yourbookpublisher.net

Distributed by:
Main Trail Productions
PO Box 365
Clearwater, Minnesota 55320 USA
320-558-6940

Library of Congress Control Number: 2004107041
Library of Congress in Publication Data
Summary: [1. Children's songs 2. Multicultural Education - Juvenile Literature
3. Multiculturalism - Songs and Music 4. Bullying in schools 5. Bullying 6. Dennis Warner
7. Beads on One String 8. Warner 9. Beads]

10 9 8 7 6 5 4 3

Every man, every woman,

boy and girl.

Beads on One String,

we're one world.

I touch, you touch,

We feel so much.

We hurt and we heal,

we know love is real.

You dream, well I dream,

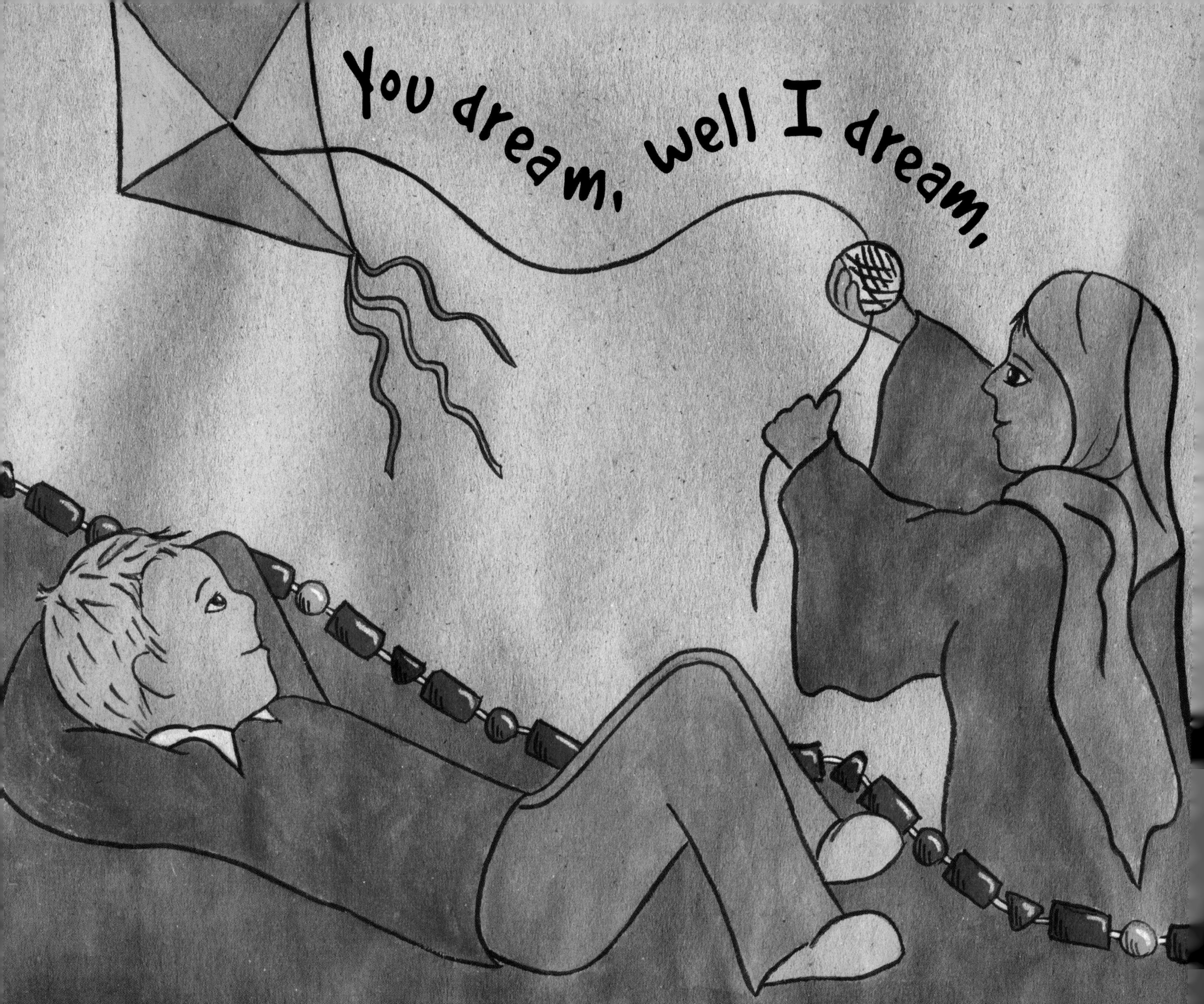

and everyone has to sleep.

We trust, we give,

We die, after we've lived.

sometimes we're gonna lose.

We're wearing

the same shoes.

We're all Beads on One String,

24

Every man, every woman, boy and girl.

Beads on One String,

We're one world.

25

Somehow we discover,

we're so much like each other.

We're all Beads on one String,
Every man, every woman, boy and girl.

Beads on One String,

we're one world ... we're one world.

29

We thought that you might be curious to know which languages the kids were speaking on page 16 (the sneezing page).

We've even added a few more examples below.

If you and your family say something different, please let us know! We'd love to hear from you.

Email: info@WarnerSongs.com

English   "Bless You"

French   "A' tes Souhait" (Ah-**tay** Soo-**hay**) "To your wishes"

German   "Gesundheit" (Geh-**zoond**-hite) "Good Health"

Japanese   The person sneezing may say "Gomennasai" (Go-men-ah-**sigh**) "I am sorry" or
                 "Sumimasen" (Soo-mee-mah-**sen**) "Excuse me" if it is a REALLY big sneeze!

Mandarin   Generally a sneeze is not acknowledged, but people from China or Taiwan may say
                 "Ni hai hoa ba? Ni ying gai kan yi sheng" (Knee hi how bah? Knee yin guy con yee sheng)
                 "Are you okay? You should see a doctor!"

Russian   "Будьте здоровы" (**Bood**-T-yeh zda-**ro**-vwee) "Be Healthy"

Somali   "Alhamdu Lalahi" (Al-**ham**-doo Lay-**lah**-hee) "Bless You"

Spanish   "Salud" (Sah-**lood**) "Bless You"

Vietnamese   A sneeze may not be acknowledged but someone might say "Ai Nhac" (Eye **Yut**) "Somebody's talking about you"